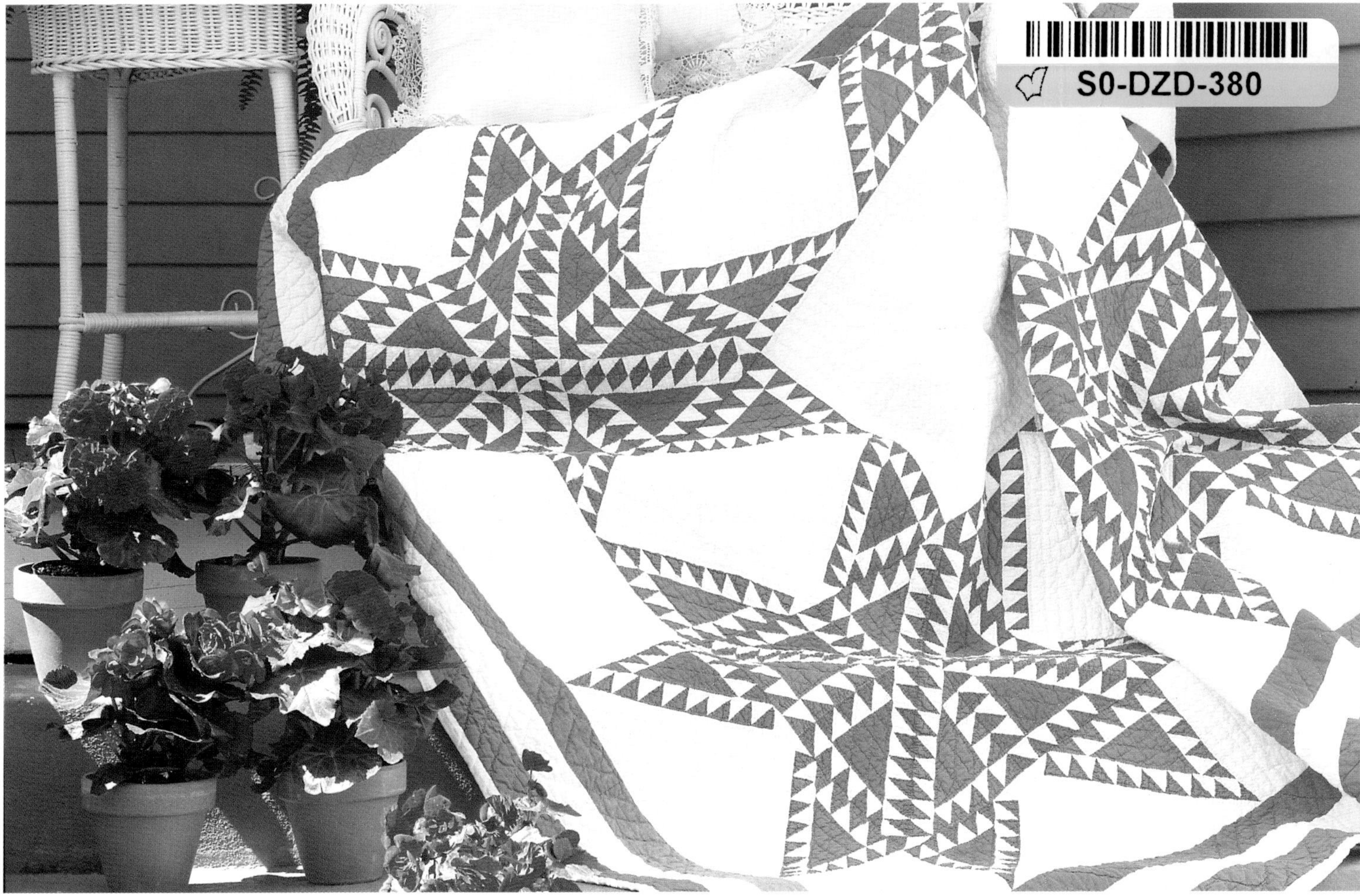

quilt

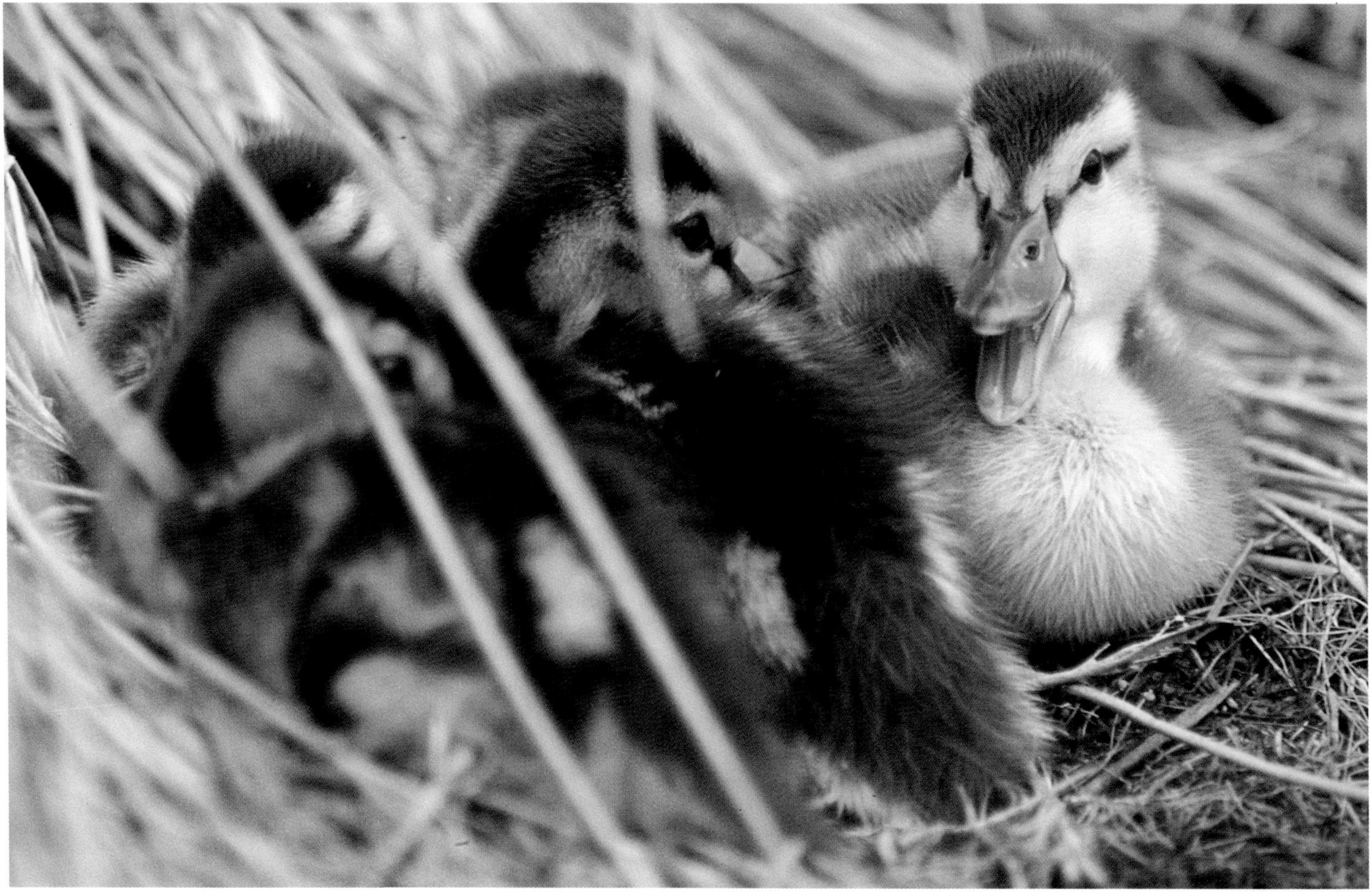

quack

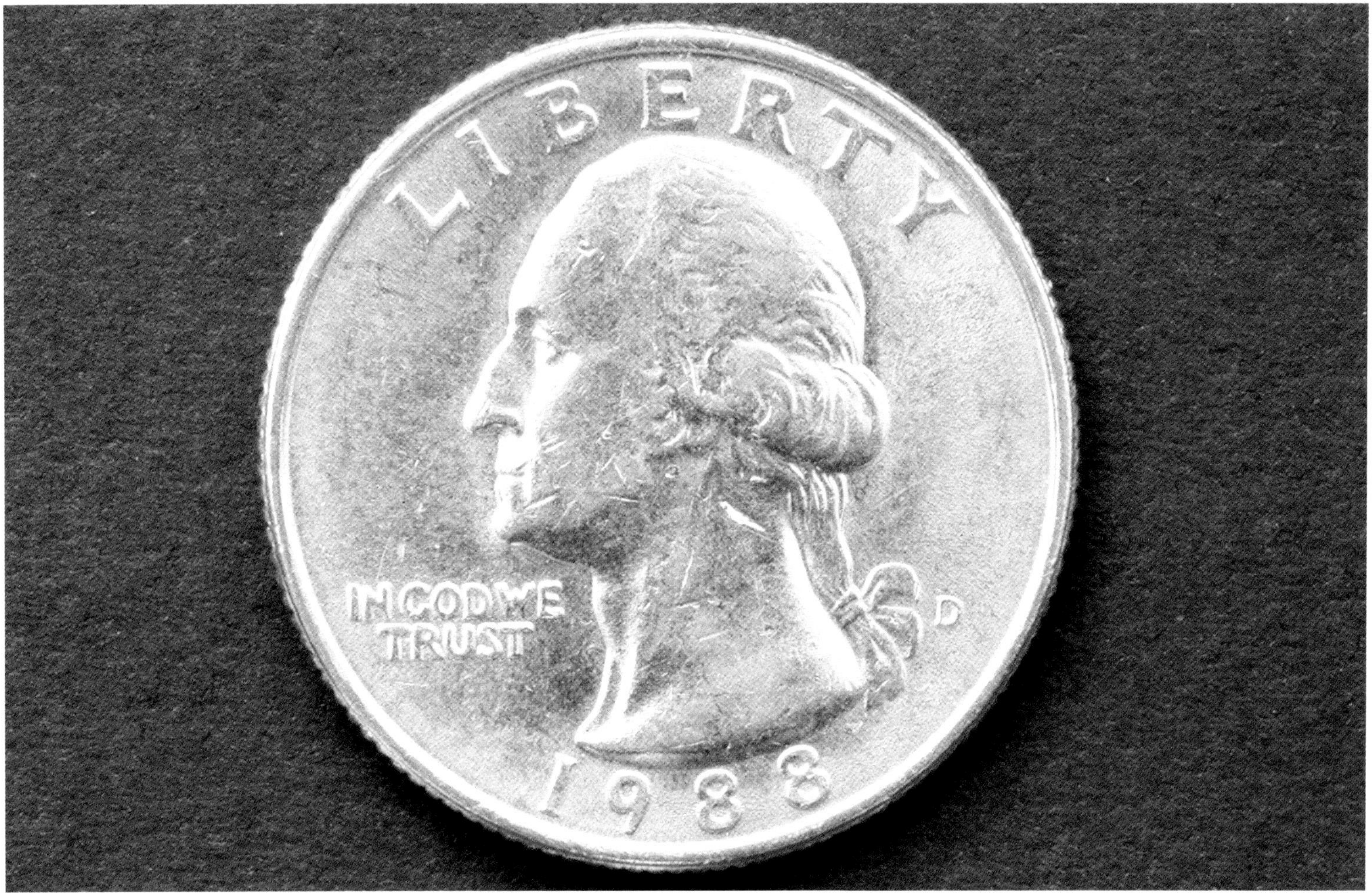

quarter

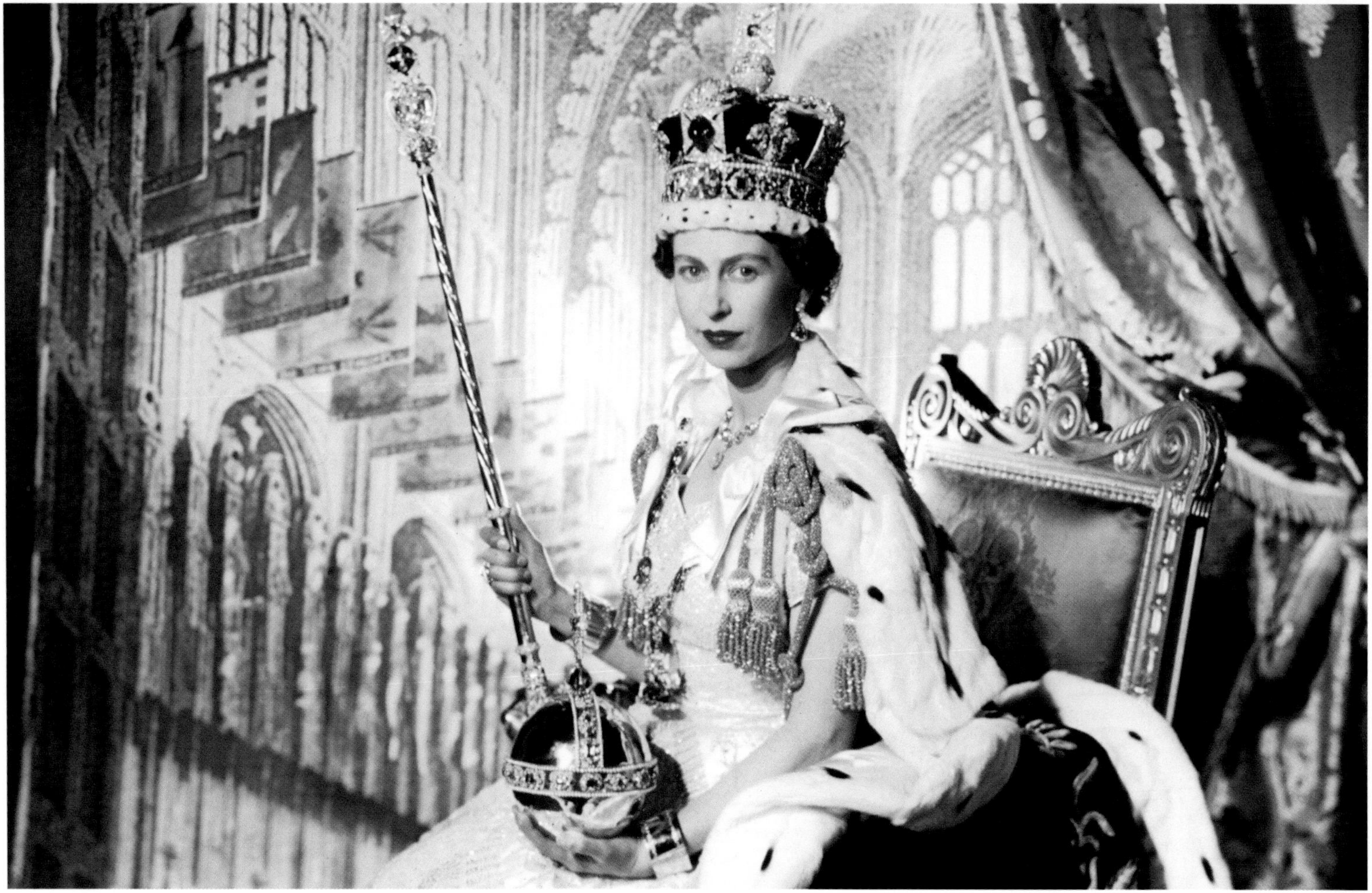

queen

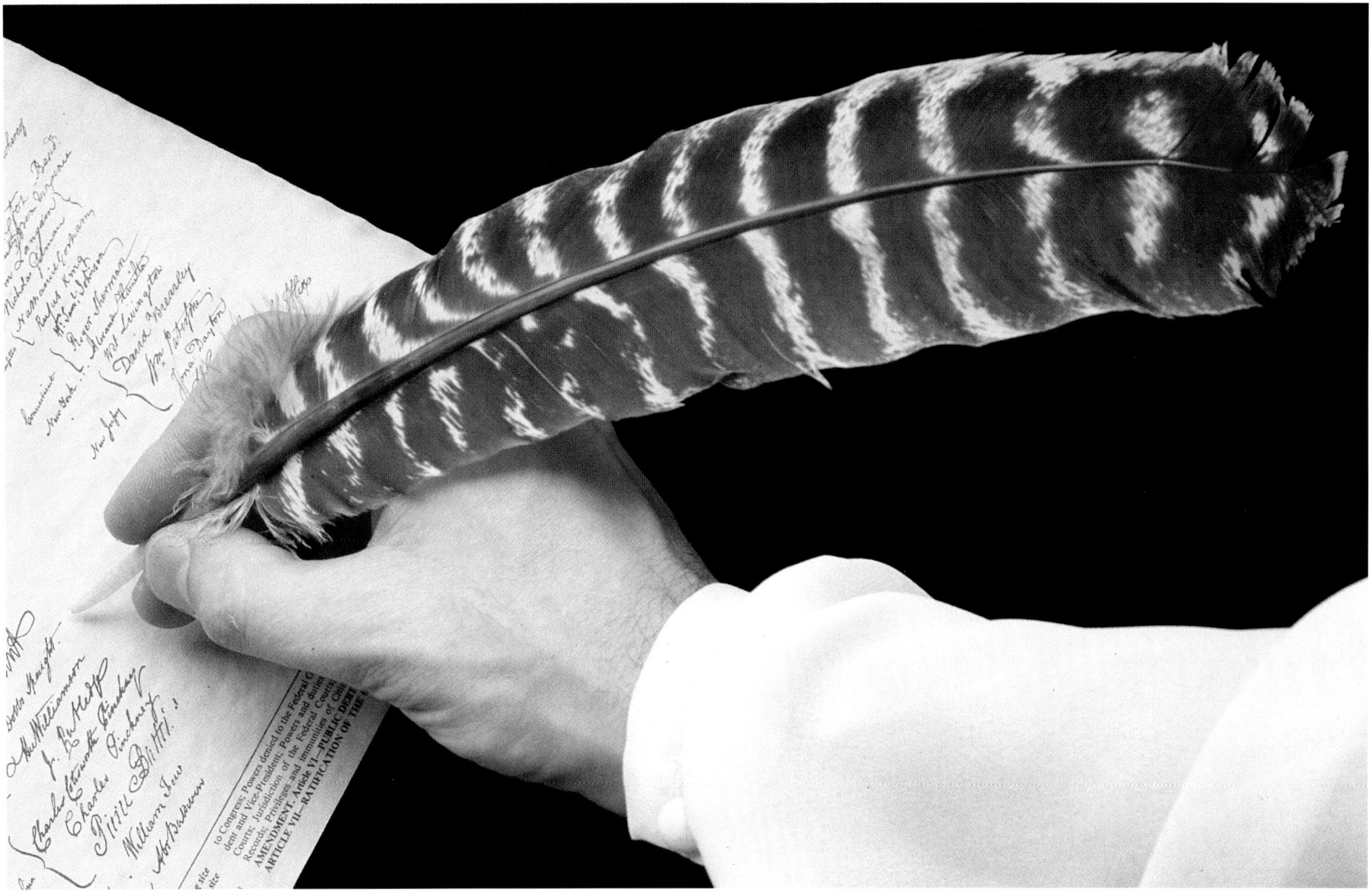

quill

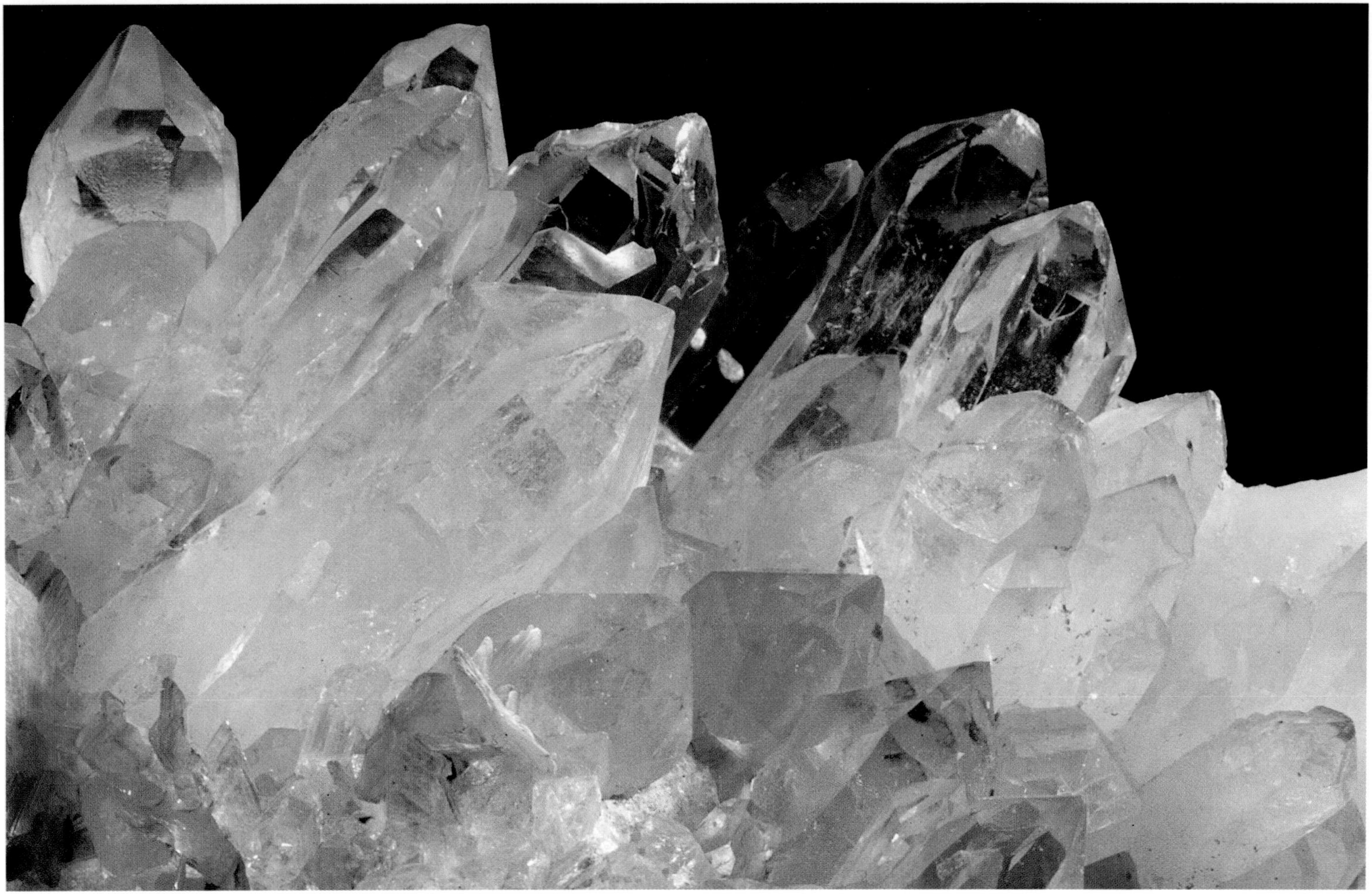

quartz

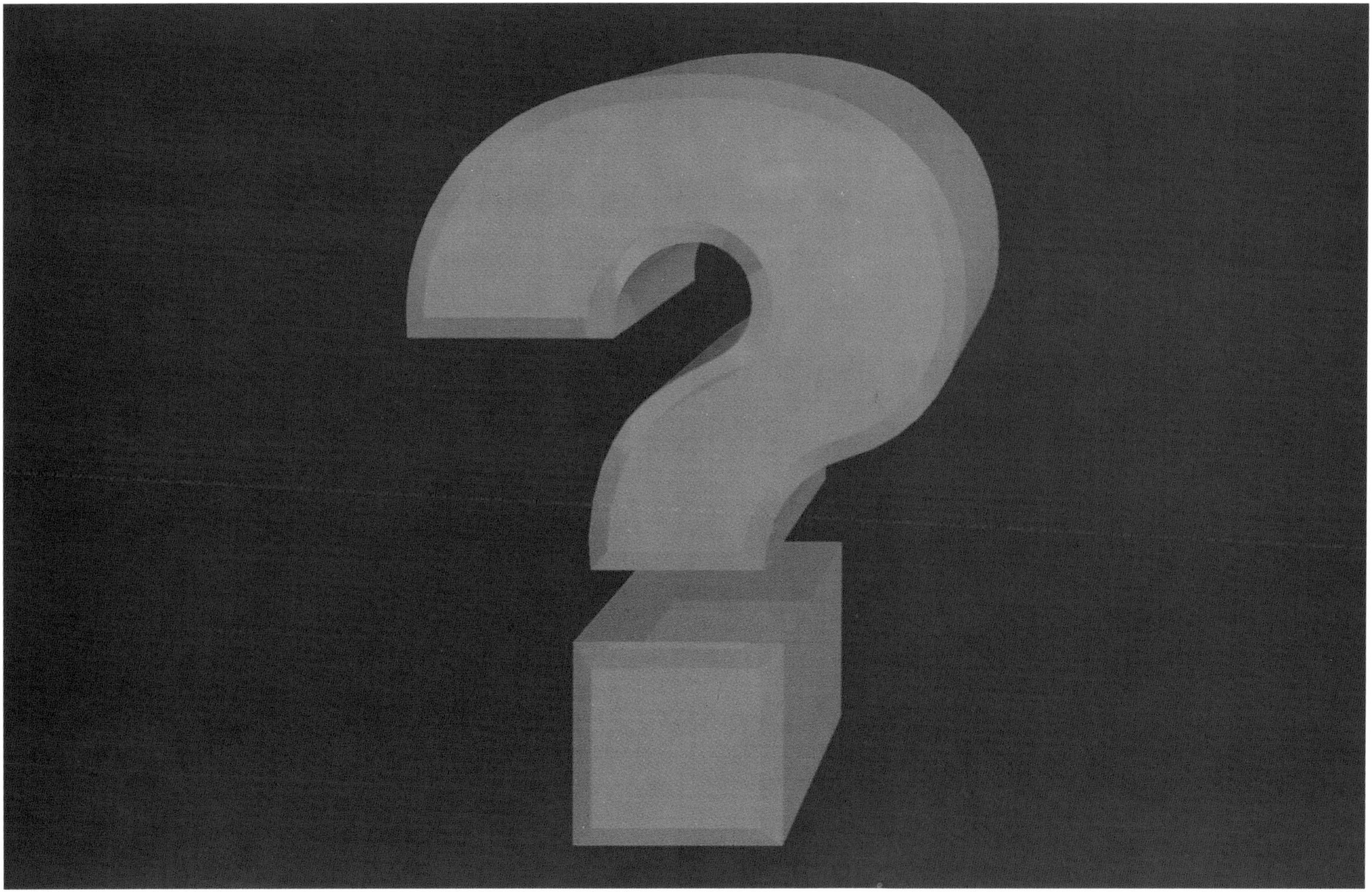

question mark

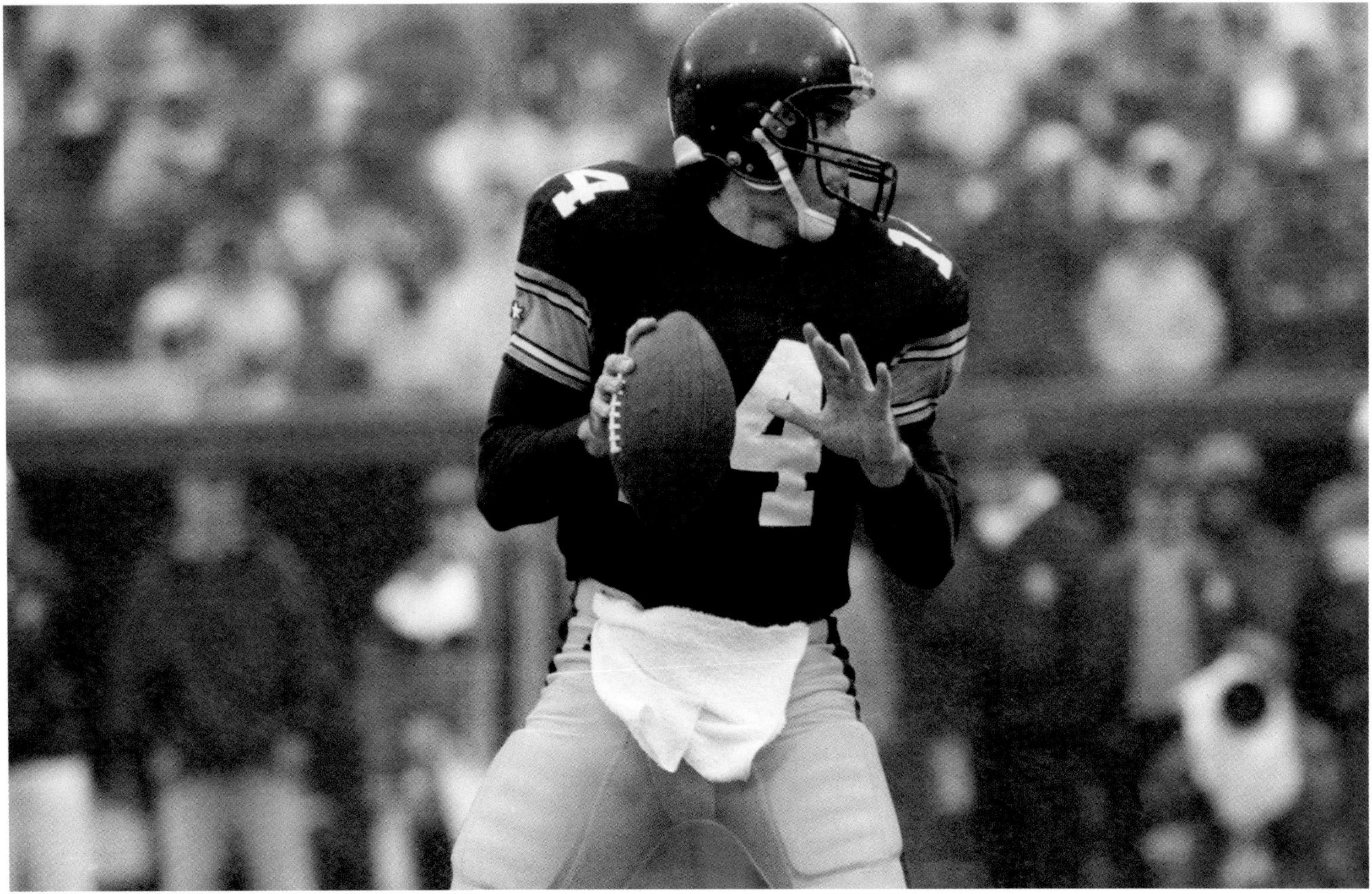

quarterback